LOCOMOTIVES THROUGH
NORTHEASTERN PENNSYLVANIA

D&H #7303 at Sunset at Tayor Yard.

LOCOMOTIVES THROUGH NORTHEASTERN PENNSYLVANIA

MICHAEL G. RUSHTON

AMERICA
THROUGH
TIME

This book is dedicated to all the people that worked in the railroad industry in Northeastern Pennsylvania. They did a dangerous job just to support their families and give them a better life.

AMERICA THROUGH TIME®
An imprint of SUTTON PUBLISHING INC.
www.through-time.com

First published 2025
Copyright © Michael G. Rushton 2025

ISBN 978-1-63499-561-0

All rights reserved. No part of this publication may be reproduced, stored in a retrieval system or transmitted in any form or by any means, electronic, mechanical, photocopying, recording or otherwise, without prior permission in writing from Sutton Publishing Inc.

Typeset in 10pt on 13pt Sabon
Printed and bound in the United States of America

CONTENTS

Introduction		7
1	End of D&H	9
2	Canadian Pacific Startup, Early '90s	15
3	Vulcan Locomotive, Previously in Downtown Wilkes-Barre	34
4	Pocono Northeast Railway (PNER)	36
5	Before the DL, There Was LVAL	41
6	Delaware Lackawanna	44
7	Conrail	54
8	Luzerne Susquehanna	65
9	LS/RJ Corman Hudson Interchange	66
10	Early Blue Mountain, Reading and Northern	73
11	Reading and Northern	76
12	Heritage Units	78
13	Steam	82
14	Classic Cab Units	93
15	Amtrak Visiting Steamtown	95

INTRODUCTION

The whole idea of this book was to paint its pages with different colored, visually interesting photos of railroad locomotives. These photos are from many years of photography. It is important to remember you don't see this variety on a daily basis.

Over the years, there have been a large number of railroad locomotives around Northeastern PA. Many of the larger railroads have power pools that can lead to a great variety of models and color schemes.

The shortlines often have a set number of locomotives assigned to them, so you see the usual suspects track side. A lot of times these shortlines have older locomotives bought second hand and pressed into service.

Sometimes railroads will make use of leased locomotives. It is just what the name implies: instead of buying locomotives, the railroads lease them—such as for periods of high traffic.

One of the first companies involved in this was the Precision National Corporation. Precision National would buy second-hand units, mainly first-generation units and cab units, refurbish them to working order, then put them up for lease.

Now and again, colorful leased units are mixed in with the regular power on many railroads.

Some railroads have been painting their motive power in old throwback paint schemes. These "Heritage" units recall Fallen Flag railroads and are favorites with railfans.

AUTHOR'S NOTE

While care has been made to correctly identify locomotives and equipment, don't get upset if I call a GP38-AC a GP38-2. If I mistake a CF-7 for anything else or a GP30-RN, well, that is an unforgivable sin. You must turn in your railfanning license for that.

Also, I take no responsibility for your actions trackside. It is very dangerous to be around moving railroad equipment. Please stay a distance from the tracks. Be aware of hazmat-placarded cars and things like metal straps overhanging from moving freight cars.

A special thanks to Samantha Whipple.

1
END OF D&H

I first got into photography in the late 1980s and early 1990s, when we were at the end of the D&H Railroad. Just a handful of the famous "Lightning Stripe" scheme units remained. Many of the "Final Dip" units remained—a dark blue carbody and yellow lettering and the shield emblem. A few times, a high hood Road Switcher all in blue was found working at Taylor Yard and on locals.

D&H LOCOMOTIVES WITH LEHIGH VALLEY MARKINGS

Below are a few locomotives with the Lehigh Valley markings showing through the flaking blue paint. D&H 7308 actually looked like a Lehigh Valley locomotive, but it was more red than blue. It was an anachronism at this point in time.

CP (DH) #7308, a GP38-2 with Lehigh Valley paint showing.

CP #7308, different pose at Taylor Yard.

D&H #7314 at Avoca, PA (later renumbered to 7308 by the CP).

— END OF D&H —

LIGHTING STRIPES AT 7TH AVENUE, SCRANTON

Two units in the D&H Lighting Stripe scheme haul a train near the former Steamtown loading platform on 7th Avenue in Scranton. They headed away at a fast speed.

Above: D&H #7309 at the 7th Avenue loading platform in Scranton.

Below: D&H #7309 and #7312 at 7th Avenue, Scranton.

GUILFORD'S BLACK PAINT

In the mid-1980s, Guilford Transportation took control of the Delaware and Hudson. Several railroads were under the Guilford umbrella. I thought it was a dull, ugly paint scheme—a gray-black carbody with a "G" logo and lettering in white or orange. When the D&H was declared bankrupt, they painted over the "G." Honestly, I only remember seeing a few at Taylor Yard. Several strings of these units were briefly at Taylor before being sent to MLK Rail in Mountaintop.

Above left: Various Guilford units at Taylor Yard.

Above right: Another string of Guilford units at Taylor Yard.

Left: These units were on their way to Morrison-Knudesen (MK) in Mountain Top for rebuilding.

— END OF D&H —

MORRISON KNUDSEN RAIL, MOUNTAINTOP, PA

This was the only time I ever visited MK Rail in Mountaintop, PA. That was on site of the former Foster Wheeler. There really was not much to see as the whole plant was fenced off.

MK got a contract to refurbish some KCS and Rio Grande units. This led to the building of this plant. A friend who just out of the Vo Tech Electrical Program had a job offer, but they turned it down because it was a night shift.

There were dead lines of Rio Grande and KCS units; on the other side, it looked like two more tracks of faded Conrail units were way past their prime. The only thing of real interest was an FP7 that was painted in Reading colors.

Eventually the work dried up there and the plant was closed. It was demolished, and as of a few years ago, nothing was on the site.

Morrison-Knudesen Mountian Top facility.

MK Mountian Top facility; a string of Conrail units.

MK Mountian Top facility.

MK Mountian Top facility; FP7 undgoing repairs.

2
CANADIAN PACIFIC STARTUP, EARLY '90S

When the Canadian Pacific came on the scene in the early '90s, a variety of locomotives came with it. They were mostly faded "Action Red" with the Pacman-shaped "Multi Mark" logo; at one point in time, various divisions of Canadian Pacific had a different color "Multi Mark" to denote its business unit.

GATX LEASERS COMMON ON CP STARTUP

At the time the CP took over the D&H, the most common power consisted of SD 40-2s. The CP could not field enough power, so every other unit in the lash ups were blue GATX leaser units. This made for colorful trains indeed. A few times, some Armour Yellow GATX units were found online. The Armour Yellow were probably ex-Union Pacific units.

CP train at 3rd Avenue, Kingston, PA.

— LOCOMOTIVES THROUGH NORTHEASTERN PENNSYLVANIA —

Above left: Two blue GATX units as pushers at Laflin, PA.

Above right: Colorful CP train at Avoca, PA.

"REDBARNS" VISIT THE AREA

That's when we'd start seeing a large variety of "Canadian Units." Some of the best ones were the "Red Barns" or the SD 40-2F Model. This was a cowl unit with a cowling covering the carbody, enclosing all the parts and protecting it from the weather. It kind of looked like a barn on wheels.

Redbarn #9023 with D&H friends at Taylor Yard.

— CANADIAN PACIFIC STARTUP, EARLY '90S —

YELLOW GATX UNIT ON POINT, PLAINS, PA

This was at the startup of the Canadian Pacific takeover of the D&H. An Armour Yellow GATX is the lead unit in this snowy scene at North River Street in Plains, PA. It was very common to have leased units mixed in with these early trains.

Above: A yellow GATX unit leads a CP train over River Street in Plains.

Below: The same yellow GATX unit just crossed "The Gauntlet" into Plains.

SOO LINE

Yes, there was a good variety in the CP Rail years. In addition to the CP Rail locomotives, we got treated to Soo Line. The Canadian Pacific in the U.S. went through a few different names. After 1995, the eastern U.S. operation was known as the St Lawrence and Hudson Railway. Several color schemes and logos were made for CP Rail too. The "Beavers" featured a beaver in the logo.

Above: A variety of Soo units in Taylor Yard.

Below: "Going away" shot of Soo units, Taylor Yard.

— CANADIAN PACIFIC STARTUP, EARLY '90S —

Matching red roadset—the stripes even match up.

Soo SD60 on display at Steamtown.

BIG TRAIN AT AVOCA, PA

I happened to be walking near the tracks. This CP train featured no less than six head-end units. One of them was a high hood cabless "B" unit with the windows painted over. It did not look like an overly large train. The extra units must have been deadheading.

Big CP train at Avoca, PA.

The red unit in middle is high hood B unit, with cab windows painted over.

Six units on the point, at Avoca, PA.

— CANADIAN PACIFIC STARTUP, EARLY '90S —

TRAIN COMING OUT OF THUNDERSTORM, AVOCA, PA

Near the same stop in Avoca, another train typical of the period came out of a thunderstorm into the sun. SD40-2s were common power. By this time, some of the CP SD40-2s were getting a little rough with faded paint and a lot of wear and tear.

Above: Train at Avoca, coming out of a thunderstorm.

Below: The usual CP and GATX units power this train.

21

A close-up of CP SD 40-2 #5677 at Avoca, PA.

ELEVEN LOCOMOTIVES IN ONE SHOT

In the mid- to late 1990s, Taylor Yard was a busy place, and often, meetings of trains would occur here, with the yard full of cars. Here we have a meeting of two trains, and there are also some locomotives in the yard. If you count those seen in the middle shot, you will find eleven locomotives together. Also, the southbound roadset was the same one as in "Big Train at Avoca, PA" photo set.

— CANADIAN PACIFIC STARTUP, EARLY '90S —

Meet at Taylor Yard, early CP, mid-1990s.

A unit in Guilford colors in the yard (Middle Top).

Eleven locomotives in one shot—count them!

CP DERAILMENT IN PITTSTON

Early into the Canadian Pacific startup in Northeastern PA, there was a derailment off Oak Street in Pittston. I went to see what was going on and was mad there were no large rail cranes to lift the locomotive back on the rails. Hulcher, with its specialized heavy equipment, re-railed the locomotive. The typical red-blue CP Rail GATX leasers were the main power on most trains. After being re-railed, notes say that the engines were idling.

Above: The derailment site off of Oak Sreet, Pittston.

Below: Another view of derailment site.

— CANADIAN PACIFIC STARTUP, EARLY '90S —

GREY KCS UNIT

This was a unique unit; I only recall seeing this one Kansas City Southern unit with grey paint on the carbody. Unfortunately, I was slightly too close to the tracks to compose the shot with accuracy, but I did get these two "grab" shots.

Above: Gray KCS unit at Avoca.

Below: A close-up of the logo on the cab.

THE SHOT THAT ALMOST KILLED ME

Into the startup of Canadian Pacific, the Delaware & Hudson line through Wilkes-Barre and Plains that had been dormant for a few years finally got trains. I carefully noted the times of passing trains to nail down a schedule.

While waiting on the berm by the trestle in North End, a train came flying by. Yes, the horn was blown at me. I jumped down the berm further out of the way. These new CP Trains were not the slow drag freights that were operated on the old D&H.

Above: The shot that almost killed me. I was not expecting such a fast train.

Below: A close-up of CP SD 40-2 crossing through truss trestle.

— CANADIAN PACIFIC STARTUP, EARLY '90S —

RED RED RED AT TAYLOR YARD

There was such a variety of color schemes and locomotives during the Canadian Pacific era at the Taylor, PA, Yard. There was Action Red (actually faded to an orange). Some units had the Pacman-shaped "Multi Mark." Each business unit of Canadian Pacific used a different color for its "Multi Mark."

There was a plain "CP" scheme—a "Dual Flags" scheme that had both the U.S. and Canadian flags on it. Also, there were "Beavers" because the older logo featured a beaver. There was a lot of variety here.

A variety of red CP units at Taylor Yard.

— LOCOMOTIVES THROUGH NORTHEASTERN PENNSYLVANIA —

A cut of four CP units sit in a snowy Taylor Yard.

#8230 is a GP9u, long hood forward. It looks like a candy cane with its all red carbody, no "Multi Mark," and safety striping.

— CANADIAN PACIFIC STARTUP, EARLY '90S —

FOGGY DAY AT TAYLOR YARD

A foggy day at Taylor Yard showed some of the variety of color schemes on the engines. A D&H four-axle unit in the "Lightning Stripe" scheme leads a group of Canadian Pacific engines in switching cars around the yard. Again, the trusty Pentax K-1000 was used.

To get the star "Lens Flare" effect from the headlight, I blew onto the lens and the breath condensed, causing the star. (This was not done in Photoshop.)

D&H 7303 leads a cut of CP units.

D&H unit on a foggy day at Taylor Yard.

The train begins to switch cars back and forth.

— CANADIAN PACIFIC STARTUP, EARLY '90S —

SOME CSX ENGINES VISIT THE AREA

In the early to mid-1990s, CSX sometimes visited NEPA, occasionally laying over at Taylor Yard. The first (new at the time) widecab locomotive I ever came across was a CSX unit on the former D&H at Avoca, PA.

The unit rounded the curve by the signal, up from the playground in Avoca. You could only see the yellow nose. I thought it was an F unit. The "new" widecabs evoked the design language of the old streamlined E and F diesels.

A CSX unit in an older gray and blue scheme at Taylor Yard.

— LOCOMOTIVES THROUGH NORTHEASTERN PENNSYLVANIA —

Two CSX units going northbound meet a train at Taylor Yard.

CSX GE C40-8W at Avoca, PA. It looked like an E or F unit from a distance. It was one of the first wide cabs in the area.

— CANADIAN PACIFIC STARTUP, EARLY '90S —

CSX CONVENTIONAL CAB UNITS AT DUPONT AND TAYLOR

Another day, while chasing a "high and wide" load from Air Products, a train with CSX Conventional cab units passed. The high and wide train carrying a heat exchanger had to wait for that train to clear before it could head up the mountain.

A CSX Conventional Cab drifts downgrade at Dupont, PA.

The marking on CSX Cab identifies this train as B36-7.

3
VULCAN LOCOMOTIVE, PREVIOUSLY IN DOWNTOWN WILKES-BARRE

This little locomotive sat in downtown Wilkes-Barre for years. I would walk past this switcher twice a day when I attended Bishop Hoban High School. The four-axle, 45-ton Vulcan was made in Wilkes-Barre. It was commonly referred to by rail enthusiasts as "The Vulcan."

Over the years, this unit sat here and was neglected, slowly rusting and deteriorating. Vandals smashed the windows and covered it with spray paint. Attorney George Spohrer wanted to restore the engine and had it moved to RMDI in former Lehigh Valley Coxton Yard (Pittston). A flood inundated the area, and in 2015, Mr. Spohrer passed away and the project did not continue.

A L&WV chapter member gave me a printout of some photos he took in 1984. Apparently, the switcher was in running condition and worked at an army depot in San Antonio, Texas.

Handwritten notes say: "Nov 1984 Last day of operation of Vulcan Center Cab at Hazle and Northampton streets, Wilkes-Barre, PA, Moving cars across Northampton Street on temporary tracks into Station Complex."

— VULCAN LOCOMOTIVE, PREVIOUSLY IN DOWNTOWN WILKES-BARRE —

Vulcan center cab switcher in Downtown Wilkes-Barre.

Vulcan with rolling stock.

4
POCONO NORTHEAST RAILWAY (PNER)

Pocono Northeast Railway was one of my favorite short lines. When Conrail cast off the Wilkes-Barre Cluster and other industrial trackage, the PNER took over. Many of the lines were in fact abandoned in place, and many have not had traffic in years.

The company only had a handful of locomotives. Nos. 1751 and 601 were painted bright yellow and green. I found out in later years that this was John Deer Green and Yellow. Who knew that these colors would look so good on a locomotive?

PNER HEADQUARTERS

The PNER had their headquarters in a little building on RT 92. There are no railroad tracks around it now, and it looks to be converted into a dwelling. At one time, all the locomotives could be found parked alongside it.

The former Montour RR #77 looked like a broken-down hulk, but it was still used and running. The Railbus was also parked by the headquarters. They wanted to use it in passenger service, but this never materialized.

— POCONO NORTHEAST RAILWAY (PNER) —

Pocono Northeast Railway (PNER) Headquarters, off Rt 92, Exeter, PA. Former Montour RR #77.

LEV2 Railbus and Switcher at Exeter, PA.

A head-end view of the railbus and switchers.

LISTENING TO THE PNER ON A SCANNER

I was heavily involved in the use of a scanner to monitor railroad, police, and fire frequencies. On some afternoons, it was not uncommon for the PNER to have three or four locomotives working the old branch lines and industrial areas and yards.

One unit would work the west side of the Wyoming Valley, down to Kingston, while another would be working the former Wilkes-Barre cluster—mainly the customers in downtown Wilkes-Barre all the way to the industrial park. Sometimes you would hear the PNER at Pittston Junction and Coxton Yard along with Conrail. It was neat to listen to. You sort of got the "big picture" of what was going on.

PNER ON OLD ERIE, IN HUGHESTOWN, PA

PNER would serve Kappa Graphics in Hughestown, PA, until the mid-1990s. Newsprint cars with big rolls of paper would be brought up on the Avoca Industrial Track, which was the former Erie. This was the end-of-track. At one time, the tracks crossed Rock Street and headed south toward Pittston and Pittston Township.

Most of the time, PNER #1751 could be found parked near the plant with a consist of boxcars. Sometimes other engines were parked here. Kappa Graphics at one time produced the TV Guide booklets, during which time it was known as SLC Graphics.

PNER #1751 wtih newsprint car, former Erie at the Kappa Graphics plant.

A close-up of Pocono Northeast #1751.

PNER #1751 looking down the old Erie toward Pittston.

PAINTING OF PNER LOCOMOTIVE AT QUINN'S MARKET

Here is a painting of PNER 1751 on the wall of the former Quinn's Market in Pittston, originally an Acme (pronounced Ack-A-Me). I worked at the Acme in Wilkes-Barre. The Susquehanna River and the trusses of the Water Street Bridge are worked into the scene.

#1751 imortalized on the ceiling of the former Quinn's Market, Pittston.

5
BEFORE THE DL, THERE WAS LVAL

Before the Delaware Lackawanna operated trackage in Lackawanna County, the Lackawanna Valley Railroad or LVAL handled rail operations.

VARIOUS LVAL LOCOMOTIVES

They had a handful of units. The ones I photographed were the "O&W" 901. The logo actually was an "L" and "V" inside the circle.

The LVAL also had a GP35 painted in DL&W colors lettered as Lackawanna Railway. This unit was often parked in Pittston Lumber, in Pittston, PA. I never caught this locomotive running or pulling a train.

LVAL #43 was an RS18 from the Roberval and Saugerney Railway in Canada. It had a strange color scheme—yellow with a diagonal stripe across the length to the carbody. There was a stylized "R" and "S" in the diagonal stripe. I caught this a few times in Duryea, PA, on the former DL&W Bloomsburg lines.

The shortline had other motive power, but I never spotted them out working or parked.

LVAL #41 at Duryea, PA, on the former EL Bloomsburg Line.

Lackawanna Railway Unit at Pittston Lumber (LVAL GP35).

LVAL #901 on display at Steamtown, Raiflest '92.

South Scranton, Breck Street, LVAL #901 and other units.

— BEFORE THE DL, THERE WAS LVAL —

PNER EX-CN UNIT, PLAINS, PA, AND HUGHESTOWN

This unit with the CN still on it worked on the Pocono Northeast Railway for a short time. It was interesting to see all the piping and strange configuration of the smokestacks.

This unit was parked in Plains, by the former United Furniture during some flooding along the Susquehanna, presumably to wait out the high water. Behind the locomotive was a spur leading to the former Prospect Colliery, which the Pocono Northeast mined to get the coal under the roadbed.

A few times the unit was used by SLC Graphics in Hughestown on former Erie trackage, taking boxcars with rolls of newsprint to the print shop.

Above left: LS #1216 waits out high water on the Susquehanna in Plains, PA.

Above right: LS #1216 on the old Erie, pointing toward Pittston and a rock cut know as "The Ciffs."

Right: LS #1216 at Kappa Graphics Plant, Hughestown, PA.

6
DELAWARE LACKAWANNA

After the LVAL era, the DL took over railroad operations in Lackawanna County. The Delaware Lackawanna is noted for using big ALCO and Montreal Locomotive Works diesels. They have shop facilities where they can repair and restore this motive power.

Two of the first units were painted in DL&W colors. Over the years, the Delaware Lackawanna has had a large assortment of locomotives. Recently they opened the Von Storch Shops at the site of the former D&H Greenridge Yard.

Above left: D-L #2461 crosses Lackawanna Avenue in Scranton.

Above right: This train has D-L #811 shoving backward at Pocono Summit.

DELAWARE LACKAWANNA STRANDED AT DURYEA JUNCTION

After Pocono Northeast (PNER) ceased operations, the Delaware Lackawanna got approval to operate the trackage. Scanner chatter led me to this scene, where I found a DL locomotive with some cars stuck in the snow near Duryea Junction.

It turns out it was double stuck. The crew was trying to clear snow and ice along the tracks, but there was no place to go. They said the Conrail dispatcher was not answering, so they could not get back on Conrail tracks to go to Pittston Junction.

In disgust, one of the crew members said they did not know what the problem was. While it was Saturday, he thought that he should have been able to reach someone. Ultimately, the train had to sit there until Monday. It made for a very nice photo in the snow though.

Above left: Railroad workers try to clear snow near Duryea Jucntion.

Above right: A D-L train working the former PNER tracks is stuck due to Conrail dispatcher not answering.

Right: Delaware-Lackawanna in a Christmas card scene.

"GREEN" DELAWARE LACKAWANNA UNITS

After some time, the Delaware Lackawanna railroad welcomed some green locomotives to its roster. By "green," we are strictly talking about those locomotives painted in a two-tone green, not clean, energy-saving locomotives.

The DL has been known for collecting and restoring various ALCO and MLW locomotives that make up their fleet. We want to see them spewing thick black smoke into the air and chugging along, almost like a steam locomotive.

The two-tone green scheme was from British Colombia Railways (later called BC Rail). A predecessor road, Pacific Great Eastern, also used green colors on its equipment.

Some of the units were in an almost inverted D&H "Lightning Stripe" scheme; others were simply one shade on top, another on the bottom. It was an attractive color scheme.

Two green units brace a unit in D-L corporate colors. #805 is an ex-BCOL unit.

— DELAWARE LACKAWANNA —

This unit is lettered for the Mohwak, Adirondack and Western.

MHWA #645 is an M420W with three sets of lights on it.

— LOCOMOTIVES THROUGH NORTHEASTERN PENNSYLVANIA —

BRECK STREET DEAD LINE

Off Breck Street in Scranton—where the original DL Shops were—is a dead line of equipment. Some are in various states of disassembly. Locomotives were cannibalized to fix other ones. Over the years, a lot of different locomotive and rail equipment was stored there.

Above: A roadswitcher on the dead line at Breck Street.

Below: Various ALCO and MLW locomotives near Breck Street, Scranton.

A high hood RS-11 formerly from the Winchester and Western Railroad.

Another high hood locomotive and rolling stock.

Former VIA FPA-4 sits in South Scranton.

— LOCOMOTIVES THROUGH NORTHEASTERN PENNSYLVANIA —

DELAWARE LACKAWANNA VON STORCH SHOPS

A new diesel shop was constructed at the former D&H Green Ridge Yard in Scranton. The DL needed more space to work on their locomotives. It was named after the Von Storch Colliery, a coal breaker complex in the Green Ridge section.

Because it is their shop facility, there is often a good assortment of locomotives and rolling stock parked in and around it.

Above: An early Alco switcher HH660 sits by the Von Storch Shops, Greenridge, section of Scranton.

Below: Newly aquired locomotives outside the Von Storch Shop; MLW636s from the WNPY RR.

This poor Erie mining unit got tagged with pink paint. Stickers on window say "Do Not Occupy."

A string of three "Pups" sit ouside the engine house in Green Ridge.

— LOCOMOTIVES THROUGH NORTHEASTERN PENNSYLVANIA —

VARIOUS DELAWARE LACKAWANNA LOCOMOTIVES

Here are some various Delaware Lackawanna locomotives. The DL and GVT Transportation have a wide variety of colorful locomotives, and two of the following shots were some attempts at night shots from a Pentax K-50 camera body.

The green and black unit was from the Adirondack Railway. It has a sharp color scheme.

The red, white, and blue former BC Rail unit appeared in the movie *Atomic Train*. The "West Rail" logo used for the movie was visible at one time on the carbody.

Above: DL #3007, an M630 sits in front of Bridge 60 Tower.

Below: This sharp green unit is a Century C424.

#2024 appeared in the movie *Atomic Train*.

A night shot of DL units laying over in Scranton.

7
CONRAIL

Conrail was the railroad everyone loved to hate, but they miss it now. It was kind of strange: it was here, but hard to see. In the late '80s to early '90s, and even into the 2000s, the railroad's movements were very sparse.

In the 1970s, while living on Kidder Street, you would see a switcher here and there. After 1976, I was amazed to see some Erie Lackawanna switchers. Another time, a newly blue-painted Conrail switcher derailed on the former Lehigh Valley almost by Union Street.

You had to be at the right time and place to catch a train. Sometimes coming from Sacred Heart Church in North End, with my grandmother, we would catch a local working the sidings in Wilkes-Barre. That was an almost regular occurrence—a few switchers in blue or black hauling a long string of cars.

The Thursday Night Switch Job from Coxton to Taylor Yard could be counted on. The cars got switched every Thursday night, whether they needed to or not. It seemed like it was the same locomotive, too.

A time or two I was driving around with my uncle, Mike Matiko, and we saw a few big trains on the Bloomsburg line heading to Taylor—a transfer job, most likely.

So, Conrail was around, but service was not frequent. It ran at odd times, much of the time at night, at least in Northeastern PA.

FORMER CONRAIL UNITS STORED AT KINGSTON

A big event took place: Out of nowhere, a cut of ex-Conrail units was shoved over the bridge at West Pittston and down the former DL&W Bloomsburg Line. These B36-7s were shoved to the end-of-track in what was once the Kingston Yard. They stayed there for a few weeks—not even a month—before they were exported out of the United States.

At the time, this was the most traffic that ran over the Bloomsburg line in many, many years. Currently, the line has been severed at Wyoming, PA, to close a hole in the Levee System.

— CONRAIL —

Above left: Ex-Conrail B36-7s briefly stored at Kingston, PA.

Above right: Ex-Conrail B36-7s in the former DL&W Kingston Yard.

Right: This long string of ex-Conrail units were probably the last pieces of equipment in the old Kingston Yard.

INTERESTING CONSIST

This consist is "One for the Ages." This will never be repeated. The head-end unit is a Conrail GE C40-8W, then two more Conrail units, and then MARC No. 59, a GP40WH-2. Next is MARC No. 64, an FL9AM still wearing Cascade Green from its previous owner, Burlington Northern. A few cars down is a Conrail Scale Car. This was from when RMDI was in operation. The MARC units were heading to RMDI. The Conrail units are likely the only units under power, with the rest deadheading.

LOCOMOTIVES THROUGH NORTHEASTERN PENNSYLVANIA

Conrail units on point of train at Duryea, PA. the head unit is a GE C40-8W.

Two MARC units in consist.

A MARC unit in Burlington Northern Cascade Green.

— CONRAIL —

Conrail scale car.

CGAL STALLS OUT IN DUPONT

In the late '80s into the '90s, the only Conrail train through Luzerne County was Symbol Freight CGAL/ALCG. That was Corning to Allentown and the reverse Allentown to Corning. (Actually, it was Gang Mills, NY.)

So, the train was on a three- or four-day schedule, meaning you might catch it twice a week, at night (maybe around 11 p.m. or 12 a.m.). If you caught the train in daylight hours, it meant it was late.

One time, I was over at a friend's house in nearby Hughestown and heard on the scanner the train was having problems. It was dusk, and it was raining. The train had stopped in Dupont, so we went to see what was going on. The crew was trying to restart an older locomotive, and we heard them try this several times, but it just would not turn over. It started raining heavily, so we left.

Later, we heard on the scanner that they had to back the train down to Coxton Yard. They split the train into two and took half of it up the mountain and half down to Allentown.

The locomotive's door opens as the crew attends to an older, failed unit.

CGAL, Corning (Gang Mills to Allentown), stalls out in Dupont, PA, during a rainstorm.

Conrail #5059—a GE B36-7 failed *en route*. The crew tried but could not start it.

CONRAIL IN DURYEA

As mentioned, Conrail trains were sort of hit and miss and not reliable for railfanning purposes. That being said, I did manage to catch some interesting Conrail motive power in Duryea.

One time during some flooding, a lash up of units were moved from Pittston Yard to high ground by the cemetery. They stayed there for a few days until the water went down.

Another time in the winter, by luck, I caught CGAL across from "The Pot Belly" bar. On the point was one of the first wide cabs in the area: a GP60M.

The last two shots are a train going from Pittston Yard to Taylor Yard for interchange. These show the old road bridge and track alignment. One unit is running long hood forward.

This string of Conrail locomotives moved to Duryea to avoid flooding.

— LOCOMOTIVES THROUGH NORTHEASTERN PENNSYLVANIA —

Above: Conrail #5556 rolls though Duryea. The crossing signal says, "No Right Turn."

Below left: Two units run on an old Bloomsburg line track alignment.

Below right: The first unit is long hood forward.

CONRAIL TRAIN STALLS AT PACKERTON

This was one of those lucky catches. I went to get photos of what was left of the Lehigh Valley Packerton car shops when a Conrail train stalled out.

Some newer wide-cab power was stopped just before the shops. It seemed that the locomotives were having issues with pumping up air for the air brake system. When I arrived, the crew was going up and down the train, double checking the air lines.

Another broken-down Conrail train, stalled by the old Lehigh Valley RR Packerton shops. I could not have staged this shot any better.

— LOCOMOTIVES THROUGH NORTHEASTERN PENNSYLVANIA —

With the front door agape, the crew tries to fix the problem.

This train is stalled in a scenic location at the end of the former Packerton Yard.

— CONRAIL —

NS DAY ONE AT HANOVER TWP, PA

The day that the NS took over, most of Conrail in PA saw a mix of power. They called this "Day One," with more Conrail blue than ever—before things were painted black.

I was riding my mountain bike along the dike in Hanover and came across this train. They were setting off cars and a unit by the old slaughterhouse near Breaker Road. For a time after that, it was a mix of blue and black on trains. The takeover made for quite an interesting time.

Above: Former Conrail and CP unit by former slaughterhouse.

Below: The leftmost former Conrail unit had already been set off.

— LOCOMOTIVES THROUGH NORTHEASTERN PENNSYLVANIA —

This CP unit was cut from train to switch. The train is headed south.

8
LUZERNE SUSQUEHANNA

After the Pocono Northeast operated trackage in Luzerne County, the Luzerne County got the Luzerne Susquehanna as the operator for the trackage. They mostly used a few small switchers.

These are probably some of the prettiest shots I ever took. LS #50 was parked on a siding near the Azek Company/Scranton Products with hoppers of plastic pellets behind it; it had just snowed the night before.

Above left: LS #50 off Davis Street, Scranton in the snow.

Above right: A close-up of LS #50.

9
LS/RJ CORMAN HUDSON INTERCHANGE

The trackage, owned by the Luzerne County Redevelopment Authority in Hudson, is an interchange point with the Norfolk Southern Railroad.

Various entities operated the trackage. The Luzerne Susquehanna ran over it for many years; it was recently acquired by R. J. Corman. In years past, this was a Delaware and Hudson branch line, and it served the Pine Ridge Colliery. It ran from Hudson Yard to the vicinity of Bowman Street and Conygham Avenue and continued south to the downtown.

At one time when RMDI (a company that services locomotives) worked out of the old Coxton Yard Roundhouse, various locomotives would be interchanged here. They would be set off on the siding until they could be put on a train on the main line and shipped to their destination.

Also, high and wide heat exchangers from Air Products in Hanover Twp would layover here, waiting for a main line connection.

— LS/RJ CORMAN HUDSON INTERCHANGE —

LS locomotive with an Air Products' high and wide load on a different day.

Opposite page: Connector track to LS/RJ Corman. PNER #1751 with high and wide load.

— LOCOMOTIVES THROUGH NORTHEASTERN PENNSYLVANIA —

CSX UNITS IN DARK FUTURE SCHEME HANDLE LAST CIRCUS TRAIN AT HUDSON

The last Ringling Brothers Circus train to come to Wilkes-Barre was handled by two CSX "Dark Future" units. It is a dark shade of blue with yellow on the front.

It really reminded me of the D&H "Final Dip" units that ran around Hudson Yard during the waning years of the D&H. During that time, the D&H tried to save money by going to a solid blue carbody and yellow lettering and nose. (It still looked good!)

The last Circus train picked up the RB&BB Circus cars off the Hudson siding, pulled them out into the Sunbury Line, and rode off into the sunset.

The last R&BB Circus train in the Wilkes-Barre Area pulls in behind CSX power.

R&BB Circus train underneath the old floodlight tower at the former Hudson Yard.

The CSX units look a lot like the D&H "Final Dip" paint scheme.

— LOCOMOTIVES THROUGH NORTHEASTERN PENNSYLVANIA —

EX-READING AND NORTHERN CF-7S AT HUDSON

One day, I was out on my mountain bike and spotted something green parked on the siding. There were two Olive Drab CF-7s with the Reading and Northern markings crossed out.

I caught the one unit in a light blue Blue Mountain Reading and Northern scheme at South Hamburg in the early 1990s, and later at Port Clinton in a green and yellow scheme.

The CF-7s were parked on the siding for a few days, and then suddenly they were gone—off to the new owners.

Two ex-R&N CF7s on the LS/RJ Corman lead. A parked red CP unit is also on the consist.

A head-end view of CF7.

70

TCB UNITS, VILX UNIT AT HUDSON

Another day when I was out on my mountain bike, I saw several bright yellow locomotives marked TCB that were parked on the siding. They were from the Texas Central Business Line. Presumably, they were visiting RMDI at Pittston, PA, for some work.

Like previous locomotives, they were parked here for a few days awaiting interchange before departing. The yellow was a very sharp color scheme—there is no crossing visibility issues for these units!

The next week, a unit lettered VILX was there on the siding. It was very rusty and in need of a paint job.

Ex-Conrail B36-7s briefly stored at Kingston, PA.

Ex-Conrail B36-7s in the former DL&W Kingston Yard.

This long string of ex-Conrail units were probably the last pieces of equipment in the old Kingston Yard.

10
EARLY BLUE MOUNTAIN, READING AND NORTHERN

Blue Mountain, Reading and Northern was the original name of the Reading and Northern. When the BMR&N started up, power consisted of CF7s, GE products (like U-boats), and some switchers as well.

The U23Bs in yellow or green paint were the most seen units when railfanning in the Pittston/Duryea/Avoca areas. There were also some similar units in Conrail blue running around at that time. The blue units were probably from RMDI.

When I went further afield to Port Clinton and South Hamburg and Temple, I encountered the CF7s and various switchers in a light blue-gray scheme.

A CF7 at South Hamburg, PA, in an early RBM&N scheme.

LOCOMOTIVES THROUGH NORTHEASTERN PENNSYLVANIA

Above left: RBM&N NW2 in the older light blue colors at Temple, PA.

Above right: CF7 #1501 now at Port Clinton in a green and yellow scheme.

Above left: Various equipment in Pittston Yard by an old sanding tower.

Above right: Early GE power in two different schemes at Tamaqua, PA.

RMDI

RMDI was a company servicing locomotives, scrapping them, and parting them out for resale purposes. They also sold and leased locomotives. They worked out of the remaining part of the Lehigh Valley Roundhouse at the former Coxton Yard (now called Pittston Yard). They used the BDLX reporting mark.

They operated from the late 1990s to early 2000s. At one point in time, there was a big dead line of locomotives, most of which were in various states of disassembly. When the company was in operation, a variety of interesting motive power moved in and out of Pittston.

11
READING AND NORTHERN

READING AND NORTHERN GETS BRIGHTLY COLORED GRAND TRUNK UNITS

The Reading and Northern got some Grand Trunk Western SD-38 units—a very colorful addition. Here they are at Jim Thorpe and Port Clinton. The constant influx of new power makes things interesting.

Ex-GT units at Jim Thorpe Station.

Above: The same colorful units at Port Clinton shops.

Below: A close-up of an ex-GT unit at Port Clinton.

12
HERITAGE UNITS

Some railroads have been painting locomotives into "Heritage" paint schemes representing predecessor railroads or "Fallen Flags." This is kind of like when the NFL makes "Throwback" jerseys.

The Norfolk Southern has painted quite a few locomotives in Heritage schemes. It was a good marketing tool to show off the railroad. Unfortunately, these units are few and far between, and I do not have the time anymore to camp trackside to wait for them. Other railroads have painted Heritage units as well.

READING

Samantha Whipple tipped me off to this train, seen here in Hudson, PA.

Reading Heritage unit rounds the curve at Hudson, PA.

— HERITAGE UNITS —

Reading Heritage unit at Hudson, PA.

CANADIAN PACIFIC

This unit was laying over in Taylor Yard in an older Canadian Pacific color scheme.

Canadian Pacific Heritage unit at Taylor Yard.

ERIE LACKAWANNA

Show here in the Steamtown Roundhouse, for Railfest 2024. She looks good on her home rails.

Erie Lackawanna Heritage unit on display at Steamtown NHS.

ERIE

Another Heritage unit laying over at Taylor Yard, in between runs.

Erie Heritage unit looking sharp at Taylor Yard.

— HERITAGE UNITS —

WABASH

Does this qualify at a Heritage unit? Before the DL repainted it, it had Wabash lettering on the side of the carbody.

Wabash lettered unit on the DL.

13
STEAM

I am too young to have grown up with steam, knowing only diesels. A few times on Amtrak, GG1s and other electric locomotives provided the power. It wasn't until a cold day visiting Steamtown National Historic Site in Scranton, PA, that I finally understood the appeal of steam. A steam engine sat on the turntable in the Roundhouse Complex, and the experience was unforgettable.

The full sensory effect of steam was on display. The smoke came up from the smokestack, steam rose and escaped from different places on the locomotive, and you could hear a gentle hissing sound of the steam escaping—plus the smell of burning coal in the firebox.

When the locomotive entered the yard and started pulling a train of coaches, all of these things were magnified, such as the "chugga chugga chugga" sound and the steam whistle blowing. It is easy after seeing that to understand the appeal of steam.

The Delaware Lackawanna Railroad has diesel locomotives manufactured from ALCO (American Locomotive) and MLW (Montreal Locomotive Works). The smoke spewing from the exhaust stacks and the "chugga" sounds evoke the memories of steam.

Unfortunately, all the labor-intensive things steam needs—lubrication, washing the boiler, dropping the ash, cleaning the firebox, and inspections—gave way to diesel motive power. Thus, there are a lot more "Static Displays" or "Cosmetically Restored" pieces than operating locomotives.

STEAMTOWN NATIONAL HISTORIC SITE, SCRANTON, PA

A good place to look at some steam locomotives is Steamtown NHS, located in Scranton, PA. There are a number of steam locomotives on display in and around the roundhouse and park grounds.

Depending on the operating and maintenance schedule, a steam engine may be operating. As of this writing, Baldwin #26 has been used on the Yard Shuttle.

In addition to this, there are steam locomotives that are not restored, which are parked in the yard in various conditions; these are still very interesting to look at.

— STEAM —

CP #2317 in a snow squall at Steamtown.

Another view of CP #2317.

THE BIG BOY

The centerpiece of the collection is one of the Union Pacific's "Big Boy" locomotives: Union Pacific #4012. It is a huge articulated locomotive with a 4-8-8-4 wheel arrangement. It was recently relocated to the opposite side of the park, and you can see it while driving in.

In 1984, the huge locomotive was moved from Bellows Falls, VT, to Scranton, PA. People remember it crossing the Tunkhannock Viaduct in Nicholson, PA, with many people turning out trackside to watch it.

For a few years, it was on display near the former DL&W Station in Scranton, which is now a hotel.

Being out in the elements caused its paint to weather and discolor, looking blue at times. The Big Boy had undergone a cosmetic restoration before being put back on static display.

A late 1980s view of the Big Boy, outside DL&W Station Hotel.

The Big Boy sits in the former Scranton yard prior to the startup of Steamtown NHS.

The Big Boy in an empty Steamtown yard; the ramp to the mall is not built yet.

The Big Boy on display after a cosmetic restoration.

STARTUP OF STEAMTOWN NHS

I was going through some old photos of the railroad equipment at the startup of Steamtown NHS in Scranton. A lot of interesting locomotives and other rail equipment were parked in the yard. Steam locomotives were among this new collection, with a multitude of different steam engines in various states of repair.

With no explanation or signage, it was all moved to the former ex-Conrail (previously Erie Lackawanna) yard. Later, when the park got up and running, some of these would be put on static display.

LOCOMOTIVES THROUGH NORTHEASTERN PENNSYLVANIA

Baldwin #26, still in black, and CP #2317 in an early version of Steamtown.

Meadow River Lumber #1, a Shay locomotive, at Steamtown.

Canadian National #5288 sits in Steamtown. The mall is under construction, and it does not look like the parking garage has been built yet.

— STEAM —

Canadian Pacific #2929 at Steamtown.

MODEL STEAM LOCOMOTIVE, OFF SCHIMPF COURT, SCRANTON

This is kind of an interesting photo, but I really have no further information on it. Driving on Schimpf Court in Scranton, there was a factory building that appeared vacant. A small area by some flag poles had been fenced off, and a small model steam locomotive was on display there.

About a month later, I drove by again, and the model was not there. No one knew anything about it. Currently the site is occupied by Noble Biomaterials.

A model steam locomotive near a factory in South Scranton off of Schimpf Court.

87

CNJ #113 MINERSVILLE, PA

Central Railroad of New Jersey #113 is based out of the Minersville, PA, Station. I got to see the locomotive when it was parked there undergoing some maintenance work, and I hope to one day catch this locomotive under steam or to ride an excursion behind it.

Above: CNJ #113 at Minersville, PA.

Below: Minersville Station, track layout, and CNJ's #113's tender.

— STEAM —

WANAMIE #9, ON DISPLAY IN ASHLEY, PA

This little locomotive worked the mines around Wanamie, PA. It was actually part of a Central Railroad of New Jersey operation. This was originally a saddle tank switcher. At some point in time, the saddle tank was removed. The weight of the water in the tank gave the locomotive traction. This unit is now on display at the Miner's Memorial Park in Ashley, PA. It is near the site of the former Huber Beaker.

Wanamie #9 at Miners Memorial Park in Ashley, PA.

TANDOOR PALACE INDIAN RESTAURANT

This is a little 0-6-0ST Switcher by the Tandoor Indian Palace Locomotive, Tannersville, PA. As they have remodeled the car into a seating area, you can actually eat in the passenger car! The locomotive was a Baldwin, from Bethlehem Steel. It worked at the Cornwall Ore Banks. The locomotive is painted in a bright green and red, presumably the colors of the flag of India.

I found this locomotive on steamlocomotive.com under the "Survivors" section. I would not have known about this locomotive if it was not for this website.

Tandoor Palace Indian Restaurant—a brightly colored saddle tank switcher, minus tender.

Saddle tank switcher and passenger car at Tandoor Palace. You can actually sit and eat in the remodeled car.

— STEAM —

READING T1S

Looking though photos and digital images to prepare this book, I came upon some images of Reading T1s. A few times I caught the Reading and Northern T1 #2102 pull into the Pittston Junction and the station.

Of course, T1 #2124 has been cosmetically restored and is on display at Steamtown NHS in Scranton. It looks good in its new paint and is in a prominent place in the park.

But sifting through old photos, this one came up, showing the T1 at Steamtown shortly after all the equipment was moved there from Vermont. This photo shows it in rough shape.

Above: Reading and Northern T1 #2102 pulls into Pittston Junction with diesels leading.

Below left: Cosmetically restored T1 #2124 at Steamtown NHS in Scranton, PA.

Below right: An earlier view of T1 #2124, before restoration and display.

R&N #425

Here we see #425 in 1993, at this time run by Blue Mountain and Reading, before the name change to Reading and Northern. Some of the people were calling this locomotive "Four and a Quarter." We see it here at South Hamburg, PA, and Temple, PA.

I took the train ride from South Hamburg to Temple. At Temple, they let the passengers disembark for a while.

#425 at Temple, PA, before the railroad was called the Reading and Northern.

#425 at South Hamburg, PA, as it is cut away from its train.

14
CLASSIC CAB UNITS

Who doesn't like a Classic Cab unit like an F, an E, a PA, or FA? These are some of the most interesting locomotives that were built and are favorites among railfans. Seeing these locomotives evoke memories of the golden age of passenger travel by rail. Models like the FT, F, or FA were early freight models. The image of an engineer climbing into a streamlined diesel cab is almost iconic.

I recall the iconic line from Superman, "more powerful than a locomotive," and envision a cab unit hauling a train as it speeds by.

Here and there you can find an operating cab unit. A lot of nostalgia is associated with them. Railroads like to restore them and use them for inspection trains or "Office Car Specials." There are also some units that are stored in non-operational state, but which are still interesting to look at.

A member of the train crew climbs into the cab of AHRS F3, in CNJ colors, at Jim Thorpe, PA.

Bennett Levin's E8 locomotive and former Erie RR E8 side by side at Steamtown NHS.

DL PA-4 190, on display at Steamtown.

ARHS F3s now in the Lackawanna RR Freight Scheme at Steamtown.

15
AMTRAK VISITING STEAMTOWN

Some interesting Amtrak equipment visited Steamtown over the years. A few times, excursions were run with Amtrak equipment to show the public what Scranton to NYC rail service might be like. I took a trip from Scranton and Binghamton and back, and it stopped just outside of the yard at Binghamton and returned back to Scranton.

I was never a fan of the GE Genesis series of locomotives. The wedge-shaped carbody seems to take design language from the F-117 Stealth Fighter or its test bed, Have Blue. They are probably very aerodynamic, even though they are not much to look at. I favor more classic locomotives, like the FP45.

Amtrak #110 on display at Steamtown.

— LOCOMOTIVES THROUGH NORTHEASTERN PENNSYLVANIA —

Amtrak #156, a GE P42DC, in the Heritage "Bloody Nose" scheme at Steamtown.

Amtrak #100 at Steamtown, painted up for the USPS *Century Express* train.

Amtrak #247, an EMD F40PH waits between runs at Steamtown.